The 2nd Battalion
Royal Dublin Fusiliers
and
The Tragedy of Mouse Trap Farm
April and May 1915

Tom Burke MBE
The Royal Dublin Fusiliers Association.

First Published July 2005
2nd Edition Published April 2006
by
Royal Dublin Fusiliers Association.
Website: www.greatwar.ie

© Tom Burke MBE 2005

ISBN: 0-9550418-0-5

This publication has received support from:
The Irish Department of Foreign Affairs Reconciliation Fund.

No part of this publication can be reproduced,
copied or transmitted in any form or by any means,
without written permission of the publishers.

€7.00 or £7.00

Design & Print
by
The Central Remedial Clinic
Desktop Publishing Training Unit,
Vernon Avenue,
Clontarf, Dublin 3,

Tel: (01) 805 7439

Fax: (01) 833 5496

email: workshop@crc.ie

The 2nd Battalion Royal Dublin Fusiliers and the Tragedy of Mouse Trap Farm
April and May 1915.

Tom Burke MBE
The Royal Dublin Fusiliers Association.

On 6 October 1914, the 2nd Battalion of the Royal Dublin Fusiliers were relieved by French troops at St. Marguerite. From there they moved north by train, truck and motorbuses with the rest of the British Expeditionary Force (BEF) in accordance with orders issued by Field Marshall Sir John French who believed that such a move would simplify his lines of communication and give him the best chance of acting against what he hoped would be a German flank around the town of Ieper. This northern flanking movement by the British was matched with a counter-flanking movement by the Germans in what became known as the Race to the Sea. By the end of October 1914, the image of the western front as we know it today, of muddy trenches and barbed wire winding its way across open fields, round towns and villages, had by default established itself in a line that ran from Nieuwpoort on the Belgian coast to the French border with Switzerland.

The 2nd Royal Dublin Fusiliers were a unit of the 10th Infantry Brigade in the 4th Division. The other battalions of this brigade were: The 1st Battalion Royal Warwickshire Regiment, 2nd Battalion Seaforth Highlanders and the 1st Battalion Royal Irish Fusiliers, better known simply as *The Faughs*.

On 14 October, the 10th Brigade occupied Meteren after a battle and on the following day they occupied Bailleul. On 17 October, the Brigade, on the right of the 4th Division, was ordered to move through Erquinghem on the River Lys to secure the large manufacturing town of Armentieres which had a brewery. At 06:30 a.m. an advanced guard from the 1st Royal Irish Fusiliers led the way into the town followed up by the 2nd Dublin Fusiliers in support. Crossing the bridge over the river Lys at Erquinghem was slow due to crowds of refugees on the roads. Around noon, as part of the battle to take the town, the advance companies of the 1st Royal Irish Fusiliers encountered a detachment of Saxon infantry who refused to surrender and bravely fought on. They were firing from a farmhouse named Farm Phillipeaux at La Ruage. Several men from the Faughs charged the front of the farmhouse but were shot down and killed at the entrance to the house. One of these dead men was Captain Carbery of 'C' Company. His remains were recovered by one of the Faughs and later buried in Houplines Communal Cemetery Extension. The farmhouse was set on fire by one of the Faughs and the Germans inside the burning house bravely fought on. In order to remove some of the cover the Saxons had inside the house, one of the Royal Irish Fusiliers officers found a party of engineers who were instructed to blow a hole in the side of the building. It seemed to work because by late evening all the defenders were killed.(1) By noon, Armentieres was in British hands. On their arrival into the town, the diarist of the 2nd Dublins wrote, the inhabitants *'were wild with joy at our entry, surrounded the troops, giving coffee cigarettes etc.'* The sight of these town folks who had lived in fear of the German occupiers of their town, coming up from cellars and out from closed rooms to greet these Irish soldiers who had liberated their town, must have given the men's morale a great boost. The people of Armentieres were obviously glad and appreciated the sacrifice these Irish soldiers made in liberating their town in October 1914.

Later on during the day of 17 October, the Dublins and Faughs encountered German snipers at the east end of the town. The Dublins were detailed to make a house-to-house search in order to flush out the German snipers. At nightfall they moved to the east of the town in continuation of a line held by the Faughs. 'A' and 'B' Companies acted as out-posts while 'C' and 'D' Companies occupied billets in the Aisle d'Etrangers. German snipers did cause casualties over the next few days and continued to do so until they were eventually rooted out by being killed or taken prisoner.

The First Battle of Ieper had begun on 10 October and ended on 11 November 1914. From Armentieres, the front line now ran northwest around the city of Ieper like a fist punching into the German lines. Apart from a brief pause on Christmas Day 1914, over the previous month or so military activity on the Western Front never ceased. During the greater part of the first three months of 1915, the 2nd Dublins remained in a triangular area with the three points of the triangle being Armentieres in the south, Ploegsteret in the north and Nieppe in the west on the road to Bailleul, a round distance of about seven miles (11 kilometres). During the night of 12

April 1915, a German Zeppelin flew over the village of Bailleul, where the 2nd Dublins were billeted. Three women, one child and seven horses were killed by the shells dropped from the Zeppelin.(2)

The biggest effort by the Germans in the spring of 1915 on the Western Front was the second battle to seize Ieper. In their opening attack, for the first time on the Western Front, the Germans used chlorine gas. The attack occurred on the Allied lines between Steenstraat on the Yser Canal through Bixschoote and Langemark to Poelcappelle. It was not the first time the Germans had experimented with chemical weapons. On 27 October 1914, in the Neuve Chapelle sector, the Germans fired three thousand shrapnel shells containing a nose and eye irritant as well as bullets. In an attack in Poland on 31 January 1915, the Germans tried the use of an improved lachrymatory (eye irritant) gas-shell that turned out to be a failure owing to the nullifying effect of the intense cold. The next attempt to use chemical weapons was on the Western Front and, owing to the German authorities failure to provide the inventor, Professor Fritz Haber, with adequate facilities for the manufacture of shells, gas cylinders were used to discharge the chlorine.(3) On 7 February 1920, Haber was indicted as a war criminal; sadly however he never stood trial.(4) Despite being dubbed by the British as '*Frightfulness*' and ' *an atrocious method of warfare*' which would '*fill all races with a new horror of the German name,*' the British used this terrible weapon in September 1915 at Loos.(5) They released 150 tons of chlorine from 5,243 gas cylinders killing 6,000 German soldiers.(6)

German prisoners taken at the end of March had revealed that gas cylinders were being brought up to the line. The information one prisoner gave was so precise that the French assumed he was a plant and ignored his warnings. (7) Following an initial bombardment by German howitzers, at 5:00 p.m. on the evening of 22 of April 1915, the Germans launched a gas attack on the Allied lines north east of Ieper. The Germans discharged 178 tons of Chlorine gas from 5,730 cylinders over a four-mile (6.5 kilometre) front. The first Allied troops hit were the 45th Algerian Division and the 87th French Territorial Division. Chlorine gas mixed with water (saliva and lung fluid) produces hydrochloric acid. Men's lungs just melted with the effects of the gas. The unfortunate French and Algerian troops, coughing blood and blinded, came pouring out of their trenches. French artillery began pounding their abandoned trenches in an effort to stop the advancing Germans. However, the gas reached the French guns and they too fell silent. In 1917, young Wilfred Owen wrote of such horror in his poem, 'Dulce et Decorum', est.

> *If you could hear, at every jolt, the blood*
> *Come gargling from the froth-corrupted lungs.*

The result of this attack was that the Germans had achieved a four-mile (6.5 kilometre) wide gap in the line, completely exposing the 1st Canadian Division's left flank, towards which the gas cloud was now rolling. Two Canadian officers became aware of the gas and told their men to urinate in a handkerchief and hold it over their mouths. Uric acid crystallises chlorine gas.(8) Weak in reserves, at 10:00 p.m. on 22 April, the German advance stopped on the southern slope of Pickem Ridge. During the night of 22 April, 1,500 Canadians counter-attacked the Germans west of the village of St Julien at Kitchener's Wood and suffered appallingly; but to their eternal credit they stood their ground in the face of gas and shellfire and they halted the German assault at a terrible price. Today in the village of St. Julien stands a memorial to the 2,000 Canadian men who died nearby in the battles that took place between the 22 and 24 of April 1915. To assist the Canadians holding the line, 15,000 British and Indian troops were rushed in.(9)

On 23 April, the 2nd Dublin Fusiliers, who were billeted in houses in Bailleul, were ordered to stand by and be prepared to move at thirty minutes notice. At 7:30 p.m. that night, the 2nd Royal Dublin Fusiliers and 1st Royal Irish Fusiliers received orders to march north. They left their billets in Bailleul and marched to billets at Westouter; their final destination was northeast of Ieper. The 1st Royal Irish Fusiliers left about an hour later at 8:20 p.m. Both battalions marched northwards towards Westouter where they billeted overnight.

At 07:30 a.m on 24 April, they marched out of Westouter towards Ieper. Their route took them through Haksken, Zevecoten, where they had a four-hour stop, and then on to Ouderdom, where they received a supply of ammunition. Their march with full packs took them next to Vlamertinghe and on then to the western outskirts of Ieper, arriving there at 8:00 p.m on the evening of 24 April. Packs were discharged and at midnight on 24 April, the Dubs marched northeast to St. Jean through the outskirts of Ieper.

At 04:00 a.m. next morning in total darkness, the Dubs took up a position west of the Wieltje - St Julien Road.(10)

At 06:30 a.m. on the morning of 25 April, the first wave of the counter-attack on St. Julien went in. It was still dark when the 2nd Dublins moved off. The 7th Argyll and Sutherland Highlanders, a territorial battalion that was on its trial that day, led the attack on the right and the 1st Warwickshire Regiment on the left. They were followed on the right and left respectively by the 1st Royal Irish Fusiliers and 2nd Royal Dublin Fusiliers. The historian of the 2nd Royal Dublins Fusiliers, Col. H.C Wylly, in his book *Crown and Company*, described the attack on St. Julien by the 10th Infantry Brigade.

> It was a desperately difficult undertaking. The night was extremely dark, the ground, which had not been reconnoitred, was honeycombed with trenches and strewn with barbed wire, and, moreover the artillery had not been able to register – that is to say, get its range of the terrain. Just before the attack was launched, word came back that some Canadians were still holding out in the village of St. Julien…therefore the place could not be shelled. The guns however opened up on the woods west of the village….. As soon as our men got out of their trenches we were met with a terrific machine-gun fire….. Our men dropped left and right, but they never wavered, and the Irish Fusiliers and Dublins, Irishmen all, fighting shoulder to shoulder actually got into the outskirts of St. Julien….The scattered ruins, the maze of trenches and the barbed wire strung everywhere, seriously delayed these two battalions and checked our advance. Two battalions of a brigade of the Northumberland Division, supporting the Dublins, lost their direction…. On the left the Warwicks and on the other flank the Highlanders got within seventy yards [*64 metres*] of the German trenches in front of the wood [*More than likely Kitchener Wood*] here they were hung up and were 'properly hammered', in the words of one who was there, by German high-explosive shells. Nevertheless, by this gallant attack the gap between the Canadians east of St. Julien and north of Fortuin was filled.(11)

Sergeant Hugh Wilson, a machine gunner with the 1st Royal Irish Fusiliers, described some of the gruesome killing of both Dublin Fusiliers and Germans. His officer had been wounded, so Wilson, being the next in charge, carried on with the attack.

> I ordered the advance, and we rushed across an open space until we came to a hedge round a farmhouse. Here there was hardly any cover so that it was a very unhealthy spot. Some of the Dublins were behind the hedge to our left and they were getting slaughtered wholesale, the enemy being only a few yards away. This hedge finished a little to the right and so I told the next senior I was going to creep along to see if I could find a position for our guns. The bullets were coming through this hedge like hail, and I as I crept along I had to crawl over the dead bodies of some of the Dublins. When I got to the corner, I saw that one of ours had been there before for he was lying dead by a tree, so I kept low and had a look around. I could see the Germans bobbing up and shooting just a few yards away and then a party of Dublins charged and it was quiet lively watching them shooting and stabbing them. They captured the trenches to our front, but the trenches on our right were still in the possession of the enemy. I forgot myself watching this affair and when I looked round I saw my men all up running to a trench a little to the left. I shouted to them and the other Sgt. shouted they had been ordered here. So I was left on my own, and being in command of the guns I had no rifle, and oh I so wished I had one for there was a German bobbing about that looked an extra good target.(12)

Later on during the fighting Sgt. Wilson was wounded in the knee and was carried back to safety by a wounded Dublin Fusilier who had been shot through the head. Sgt. Wilson was taken back to an aid post, his fighting days were over. He died in 1947 aged sixty-two. At the end of the day, i.e. 25 April, the Dublins dug themselves in on a line that was roughly 400 metres from St Julien. Their Commanding Officer, Lieut.-Col. Arthur Loveband, was wounded in the hand. Their comrades in the 1st Royal Irish Fusiliers lost one of their brave and decorated men, Private Robert Morrow, who died of wounds received during the day. Thirteen days earlier, Private

Morrow had won the Victoria Cross for rescuing wounded men under German shellfire near Messines. His name appeared in the *London Gazette* on 22 May 1915.

On 4 May, the 2nd Dublins were withdrawn from the line and took up camp round the Chateau des Trois on the east bank of the Yser Canal about half a mile north of La Brique. They arrived there at about 2:00 a.m. on 5 May and were greeted by single German aircraft that dropped two bombs slightly wounding two men from the battalion. The following two days were quiet. (13) Over the previous days, German aircraft were used to spot British trenches. When located, they dropped smoke-balls to locate the British trenches for their artillery to launch an attack. (14) Between 26 April and 4 May, the Dubs along with the rest of the 10th, 11th and 12th Infantry Brigades, holding the line in front of St. Julien down to Fortuin, were regularly shelled by the Germans both day and night often using gas shells. The diary of the 1st Royal Irish Fusiliers described those few days and nights as *'a continuous nightmare.'* (15)

On 2 May, the Germans launched another gas attack from St. Julien on the lines occupied by the 10th, 11th and 12th Brigades; however the men had been supplied with respirators *'of a sort'* and the attack failed to breach the British line. (16) The '*sort*' of gas mask the Royal Irish Regiment used was simply a piece of moistened flannel.(17) The entire Ieper salient came under a *'never ending deluge of heavy projectiles.'* (18) The men in the front lines must have lived through hell itself. The 2nd Dublins were not relieved by another battalion, they were in fact ordered back beyond a new line about 400 meters from the line they had dug on the night of 25 April. The Commander of the British Expeditionary Force, Sir John French, believed his position was too exposed and ordered General Plumer, who was charged with the defence of the Ieper salient, to withdraw his men to a prepared position. So, after fighting their way up to the outskirts of St. Julien from St. Jean, and in the process losing a lot of men, the 2nd Dublins were then ordered back east of St. Jean from where they roughly began.

The surprise and devastation the Germans achieved by the use of gas on 22 April did not achieve its full potential in capitalising on the ground lost by the Algerian and French Divisions. The German Command had little trust in the value of gas. There were no reserves at hand to pour through the wide gap that had opened in the Allied lines following the gas attack on 22 April. Between 24 April and 5 May 1915, a total of 137 men from the 2nd Battalion, Royal Dublin Fusiliers, were killed in action or died of wounds. On 25 April alone, the 2nd Dublins lost seven officers and forty-three other ranks killed.(19) The 1st Royal Irish Fusiliers suffered somewhat similar numbers. They lost three officers and forty-five other ranks killed.(20) For roughly the same period the 2nd Royal Irish Regiment suffered a loss of twenty men killed in action or died of wounds. The 1st Royal Irish Regiment, who was stationed in the same area near Wieltje, again for the same period, suffered a loss of one officer, 2nd Lieut. C.R. Fausett, and thirty-eight men of other ranks.(21) The 10th Infantry Brigade suffered more casualties than any other unit having lost sixty-three officers and 2,300 men of other ranks.

Amongst the Dublin's casualties there was three eighteen-year-old young men that died. They were Lance-Cpl. Peter Galvin from No. 7 St. Peter Street, the Coombe, Dublin. Lance-Cpl. Albert Gordelier from Bermondsey in Surrey and Private Thomas Clinton from Navan, Co. Meath. All three of these young men's bodies were never found and their names are on the Menin Gate, Panels 44 to 46. The oldest Dublin Fusilier who died was Pte. Peter Farrelly from Manchester. Peter was forty-seven. All of the men mentioned above are listed on the Menin Gate in Ieper. Perhaps it is an indication of the ferocity of the German shelling, that the majority of the men's bodies that died were never found.

Out of the 137 dead Dublin Fusiliers, 117, or 85.5% of them are on the Menin Gate, Panels 44 to 46. Whole families from Dublin were destroyed with grief. Among the dead Dublins were two brothers from the fishing village of Skerries in north county Dublin. Private Joseph Gossan from Strand Street in Skerries was thirty years of age when he died of wounds on 27 April. He is buried at Wimereux Communal Cemetery, Grave Reference IF5A. His brother James died of wounds a few days later on 4 May. James was a married man aged thirty. Together with his wife, Mary Ellen, they lived at No. 30 Church Street, Skerries, Co. Dublin. James is buried at St. Sever Cemetery, Rouen, Grave Reference A825.(22) Another Dublin family who suffered was the McDonnells from the heart of Dublin's inner city, commonly known as The Liberties. The first member of the family killed with the 2nd Dublins on 26 April was Pte. Peter McDonnell. Peter came from No. 46 Bride Street and was forty-two when he was killed in action. Sadly, his two brothers, Patrick aged thirty-two and John aged twenty-two who served in the 2nd Dublins, would die roughly a month later in an even worse German gas attack.

Pte. Hugh Lynch, 2nd Battalion Royal Dublin Fusiliers, was born at No. 67 Railway Street in Dublin in 1896. He came from a family of six children. His father's name was John and his mother was Mary Weldon. She too was born and reared in Dublin's north inner city. The family moved to No. 61 Foley Street Buildings. Hugh, like hundreds more young men from the inner city, joined the Dublin Fusiliers. He joined about a year or two before the Great War began, during the General Lockout, when there was little or no chance of obtaining work. By family memories, he was a very quiet lad. On 24 April 1915, Hugh died of wounds. He was nineteen years of age. His nephew, also named Hugh Lynch, lives in Artane, on the north side of Dublin city. For years, at the request of his mother, Hugh's family kept his Death Scroll wrapped in a scroll dedicated to the Sacred Heart. Hugh's body was originally buried in Westroosebeke Cemetery. The Cemetery was destroyed in later battles. A headstone marked; *'To the memory of Private H Lynch'* now stands in the Divisional Collecting Post Cemetery, Westroosebeke Communal Cemetery. For the first time since the lad died, in February 2001, a wreath was placed on his grave by a young Belgian man on behalf of Hugh's family who live in Artane, Dublin.(23)

Between 8 and 12 May, the 2nd Dublins occupied a sector which covered a distance of about 100 yards (91 metres), between Shell (Mouse) Trap Farm, and west of the Wieltje-St. Julien Road. During this time they were continuously shelled and sniped at. The land around the farm was like the surface of the moon with shell craters. Battalion headquarters was at Wieltje Farm House. Mouse Trap Farm was a Flemish Chalet situated on a ridge known as Bellewarde Ridge. From the Menin Gate, it is about two and a half miles (3.2 kilometres) north-east of Ieper. It was located where the front line took a right-angled bend in the Ieper salient.

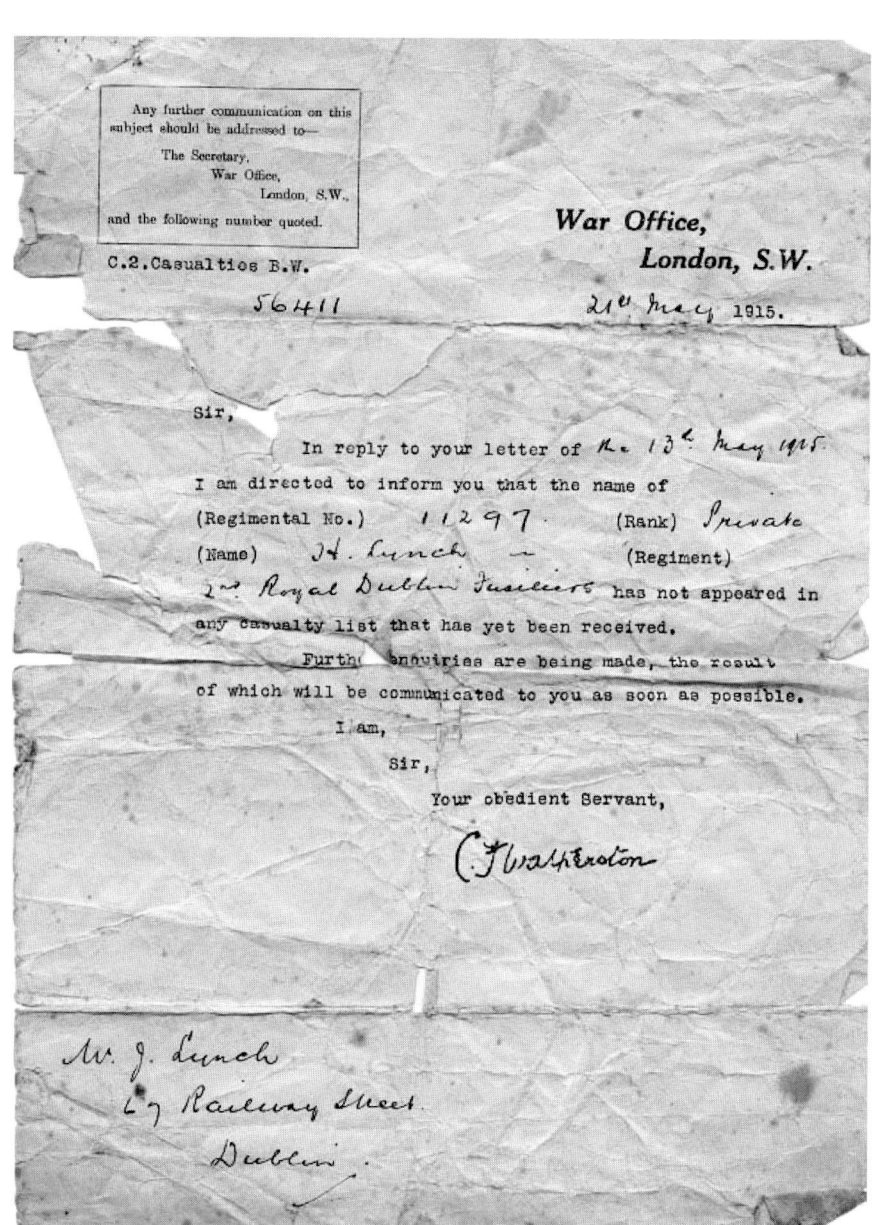

Letter from the War Office in London to Mrs. Lynch, telling her that her son was missing.

Parchment upon which Mrs. Lynch placed the paper cutting referring to her son's death.

The Sacred Heart Parchment in which Hugh's mother wrapped the Parchment.

The Headstone of Private Hugh Lynch 2nd Royal Dublin Fusiliers at the Divional Collecting Post Cemetery, Westroosebeke Communal Cemetery.

On the evening of 12 May, the 2nd Dublins were relieved by the 15th Hussars and London Rifle Brigade, and marched back towards Ieper to bivouac in the grounds of Vlamertinghe Chateau. Over the next twelve days they served their time in and out of the trenches, regularly being shelled and sniped at from the Germans in St. Julien which lies about one and a half kilometres northeast of Mouse Trap Farm.

At about 2:30 a.m. on Whit Monday, 24 May 1915, Colonel Loveband, who by that time recovered from his wound suffered back in April, along with his second-in-command, Major Magan, Medical Officer Major Russell (R.A.M.C) and Captain Tom Linky, the Acting Adjutant of the Battalion, were sitting in their headquarters dugout which lay about 400 yards [365 metres] behind the first line of trenches. Other than a German aircraft flying over Mouse Trap Farm the day before, things had been quiet enough when night fell on 23/24 May. Colonel Loveband and his officers had just finished a meal. Previous to their meal, he and Major Magan had conducted a tour of inspection of the Dubs front-line trenches in and around Mouse Trap Farm. Taking the farm as the middle of the line, to the left was the 2nd Royal Irish Regiment. To the right of the Farm was the 2nd Dublins. On the Dublins right was the 1st Royal Irish Fusiliers, amongst whose officers was 2nd Lieutenant Hugh Patrick Shine from Dungarvan, Co. Waterford. Behind the 2nd Dublins were the 9th Argyll and Sutherland Highlanders. During his rounds of the trenches, Loveband had warned all Company Commanders to keep themselves in preparation for a gas attack. The medical officer, Major Russell, had inspected all the Vermoral sprayers and warned each company about keeping their respirators damp. Vermoral sprayers were used to neutralise any gas that hung in the trenches. The battalion had ten sprayers in working order, one with each machine-gun and the remainder distributed along the trenches.

Capt. Linky and Col. Loveband were standing outside the door of their dugout when, at about 02:45 a.m., they saw a red light fired from the German lines to the north-west of the farm and immediately followed by three more red lights directly over Mouse Trap Farm. More red lights were seen over the German lines south-east from where Loveband and Linky were standing. Within seconds of the final red light going up, a dull roar was heard - *'more of an explosion (certainly not a shell) and we saw the gas coming on either side of Shell Trap Farm.'* Loveband shouted to his men. *'Get your respirators boys, here comes the gas.'* (24)

In the trenches, *'Stand To'* was just over and rum was being issued. The battalion strength in the line was seventeen officers and 651 men of other ranks, i.e. 668 men.(25) Everyone was awake when the dense gas came in on a gentle north-easterly breeze.(26) Due to the nature of the ground that was a gradual slope from the direction of the gas cloud, and first line of trenches in front of the 2nd Dublins battalion headquarters, a distance of about 400 yards [365 metres], the toxic cloud took three quarters of an hour to pass over the Irish lines. As soon as the gas came over, the men came *'pouring out of the trenches'* to the left of the farm, i.e. the Royal Irish Regiment trenches.(27) *'Dropping like flies'* was the term used to describe the unfortunate Highlanders trying to evacuate their lines.(28) One cannot even imagine the agony those men must have suffered in trying to escape from the effects of the gas. They didn't stand a chance. The Germans, grey-coated storm troopers of the 51st Reserve Division, advanced immediately behind the gas cloud, bombing and bayoneting the men in the trenches. By 04:45 a.m. the Germans had captured Mouse Trap Farm and had occupied the Royal Irish Regiment trenches.

Following the gas, at about 05:55 a.m., came their artillery *'heavies'* and gas shells. Machine-gun fire was now coming from the Germans' new positions in the Royal Irish trenches left of the farm. By this time there were few left of the men who had 'stood to' earlier on in the morning. Yet, some of the Dublins did manage to fight back. They were assisted by men from the 9th Argyll and Sutherland Highlanders. The last message Captain Basil Maclear sent was: *'Very many of our men are surrounded. We must have reinforcements.'* He was killed leading a grenade assault on the occupied Dublins trenches facing the farm. His brother officer 2nd Lieut. Kempston got another note through to battalion headquarters: *' For God's sake send us some help. We are nearly done.'* At 12:45 p.m., the only surviving officer of the 2nd Dublins, Captain Tom Linky, sent a note to the headquarters of the 10th Infantry Brigade: *'Reinforce or all is lost.'*(29)

Although born in England, Basil Maclear spent much of his life in Cork. He was a fine rugby player and played as a three-quarter for his club Cork County. Regardless of the fact that he was born in England, because he lived in Ireland for so long made him eligible to play for the men in green. Basil played international rugby for Ireland eleven times. In 1906 he played on the wing and was part of the team that beat Wales in Belfast by eleven points to six. The win enabled Ireland to share the Championship with Wales. In his book, *The Men in Green* first published in London in 1973, the Irish Rugby correspondent Sean Diffley noted about Basil Maclear.(30)

> Maclear played both centre and wing. He was a most fastidious looking character who often wore spotlessly white gloves on the field. This eccentricity, however, did not conceal some very fine football ability. He was very fast and dashing, possessed a good swerve and was a noted tackler. Maclear was one of the glamorous figures of rugby at the time. He came on the international scene with a very high reputation but one contemporary account, while conceding that he was an outstanding three-quarter, rated him behind Sam Le and George Stephenson. (Note. Maclear was one of eight Irish International Rugby players that died in the Great War).

Standing at the back of his dug out, Col. Loveband was shot through the heart. (Another account stated he was shot through the head) *'The bullets came from behind '*. Another officer named Burt Marshall was hit in the shoulder by fire *'coming from the same direction.'*(31) There are some interesting questions surrounding the death of Col. Loveband. He was standing at the back of his dug out when *'the bullets came from behind'*.

One might logically assume the Germans were in front of him and his own men were behind him. If that was the case, was he shot by his own men? Why did the wounded Burt Marshall race *'off to stop the firing?'*, who was Marshall trying to get to stop firing? It certainly wasn't the Germans.

His death may well have been a tragic accident. It seems he was well liked and admired by many of the men who served with him. The only officer left with the battalion when they were finally taken out of action was Captain Leahy. It was he who wrote the account published in the battalion's history written by Col. H.C. Wylly C.B. One of the Dublins' senior officers who died that dreadful day was Major Digby Johnson from 'C' Company. Johnson's wife wrote a letter of condolence to Mrs. Loveband soon after her husband's death.

Lieutenant-Colonel Arthur Loveband C.M.G. killed in action 24 May 1915.

My Dear Mrs Loveband,

You don't know how pleased I was to get your letter. I have thought of you and would like to have written, but didn't know your address and didn't quite like to write. Digby had such a great admiration for your husband and always said how splendid and cheerful he had been all through the winter and in that action on April 25th when both your husband and mine were wounded. When Digby was home on a weeks leave, as he wasn't fit to go back, he said how splendid your husband had been in that action. Instead of being at the back as he ought to have been, he was going from Company to Company with just a cane in his hand. How proud you must be of him. I had a typed written statement from Major Magan (Second in Command of 2nd RDF) telling me all he knew. I gather the Regiment had only, on the 23rd, moved into these special trenches although they had been in trenches for 9 days and ought to have been relieved the day before – on the evening of the 23rd. Your husband and others, as Captain (Leahy) says in his letter, went round the trenches. Your husband was very dissatisfied with the position of the whole place as the trenches were not completed. Your husband, Major Magan, an R.E. and Digby reconnoitred in advance of the farm and were heavily fired on but took cover in a shell hole and got away one by one. Then came the awful gas attack next morning that Captain Leahy describes. As far as I can gather, my husband must have died about 5 in the morning, but I don't think Colonel Loveband could have known of it, and it was a man who crawled in later in the day that brought the news. They speak of Digby as having done so well and rallied his men so splendidly that morning and I am so proud Mrs. Loveband, but yet it breaks one's heart to think of it all. That splendid battalion I like to think of them as all together now. No work they did on earth wasted, but called away to some higher work, but thank God is a place where there is no more pain and suffering. What a passing it must have been. Going back to Major Magan's letter I quote, in his own words what he says of your husband's death. 'By God's blessing he had been killed instantaneously by a bullet through the brain – the bravest, the kindest hero that ever lived and to the Regiment and to his friends and to all who knew him, an irreparable loss. In every one of his actions in every hour of his life since he took command he was an outstanding example of a most heroic and wise Commander. From the time he took over from the Seaforths he had done all that was possible to make a hopeless position tenable.' It is splendid praise isn't it and to feel that your husband was so loved by them all must be a real help to you. When you write of Lettie it reminds me so of what Daisie said to me. I think it is put into their hearts to comfort us and what I should have done without the children I do not know, although the boy is only 3 and doesn't understand. Major Magan said Digby realised the gravity of the position but was perfectly calm and collected – this was the night before, then the next day, Moran, who has since died, came in and said Digby had hung on to the fire trench (first trench) for about two hours and then fallen back to support trench, where the Regiment was there, they all died to the last man. I think now I have told you all I know Mrs. Loveband. As you say, we must try and be brave for their sakes and leave them in God's care. If you ever come over to England I should love to meet you. I would come up to Town or if you could come down and spend a night or two with me. I feel there is such a bond between us widows. I am returning captain Leahy's letter. I took a copy of it, I hope you don't mind, but any news of that awful day is precious. Thank you again so much for your letter, if you should hear anything more I should be grateful if you would let me have a line, you know how one longs for news. (32)

Regardless of who killed Col. Loveband, he was now one of the dreadful statistics of that terrible German attack on 24 May 1915. Although his body was recovered and more than likely given a proper burial, the chances are his grave, like thousands of others, was ruined by subsequent fighting in the region, Consequently his name, along with the rest of his battalion that were killed that day, is on the Menin Gate. There is also a small memorial to him in St. David's Church of Ireland in Naas, Co. Kildare. The Germans had taken Mouse Trap Farm and had pushed the Irish lines back by about 200 yards [182 meters] From about 2:30 p.m. there was no fighting in the Dublin, or Royal Irish trenches. *'Everyone held on to them to the last. There was no surrender.... They all died fighting at their posts.'*(33)

At 9:30 p.m., Captain Linky received a message to withdraw his battalion headquarters and all his men to the Brigade Headquarters on the west bank of the Yser Canal. He took twenty men with him to camp about one and a quarter miles (two kilometres) west of La Brique. Out of a battalion strength of 668 who 'stood to' earlier on that morning, 647 were killed, wounded or missing. The 2nd Royal Irish Regiment also lost their Commanding Officer, Lieut.-Col. R.G.S. Moriarty, along with sixteen other officers and 379 men of other ranks.(34) The youngest recorded soldier that died fighting with the British Army in the Great War was a private with the 2nd Royal Irish Regiment. He was Pte. John Condon aged fourteen from the Ballybricken area of Waterford City. He died at Mouse Trap Farm on 24 May and is buried at Poelkapelle Military Cemetery. No doubt there were many more John Condons who died in that terrible war but who were never recorded. Between 25 April and 25 May 1915, according to the Battalion War Diary, the 2nd Dublins suffered the following losses.(35)

Officers Killed.	24
Other Ranks Killed	103
Officers Wounded	14
Other Ranks Wounded	291
Officers Missing	2
Other Ranks Missing	1,094
Total Loss to Battalion	**1,528**

According to the Commonwealth War Graves Commission records and Soldiers Died Series 76, the number of other ranks who died during that period was 383. The difference between the Battalion Diary and CWGC figures, i.e. 103 and 383 respectively, is 280. This figure of 280 would make up some of the 1,094 other ranks that were missing. The final number of other ranks who were missing is therefore 814. Of the 383 other ranks who died during that period, 323 were Irish-born, i.e. 84.3 %. Forty-two were English born, twelve were Scottish and one each was born in Wales, Australia, Brazil and Pakistan. There were two who had no place of birth data. In terms of the 323 Irish-born Dublins who died, 234 were born in Dublin, i.e. 72.4%. In terms of the Battalion, 61.8% of the men were born in Dublin.(36) These are mere statistics; each number represents a human being. It is a fact we sometimes forget.

What the statistics never show is the number of men who died after the war with illness related to those gas attacks. Moreover, statistics never show, or can we even imagine, the terrible death and suffering those unfortunate men on both sides went through dying from the effects of gas. On 15 June 1989, Jack Campbell, an Irish veteran of the Great War, was interviewed by Michael Lee, a TV cameraman from the Irish Television station, Radio Telefís Eireann (RTE). The interview took place at Jack's hospital bed in Leopardstown Park Hospital in Dublin. Jack was a regular soldier who served in the Black Watch and during his interview he spoke to Michael about gassed men around him pleading with him to shoot them and put them out of their misery. ' *It takes up to three hours to die from gas.*' Jack said to Michael. *'Yes, it's been said to me and others, for Christ sake be a pal and put one in to me and finish me.*'(37)

One of those men who was gassed at Mouse Trap Farm was Pte. John Smith. His lungs were so badly damaged that he was sent back to Ireland to recover. His trip home in 1915 ended on a happy note. In December that year, he married a young lady by the name of Helena Mary Loan, a children's nurse from Bray, Co. Wicklow, where the couple were married. John recovered somewhat and returned to his battalion. Helena went to work looking after wealthy children in England. John was gassed again, exactly where and when is not known. This time however his weakened lungs gave in altogether. He was sent back to Ireland again and spent some time recovering at the Irish Counties War Hospital (now offices of the Irish Dept. of Defence) on St. Mobhi Road in Glasnevin, Dublin. In 1917, John was awarded the Military Medal. His name is recorded in the *London Gazette* on 19 November 1917. John Smith survived the war and returned a damaged and weakened man to his wife Helena. On 10 March 1919, John was honourably discharged from the army. Helena and John obtained a house on the Claremont Estate in Glasnevin, Dublin. He was a terribly weakened man. The gas attacks he had come through had left their mark. He got a job in Jamesons, the whiskey distillers in Dublin. In April 1920, John and Helena's first child was born, a little baby girl they named Helena. John's mother was named Rachel, and Helena's mother was named Elizabeth, and so Helena was christened Helena Elizabeth. Today she is known to her friends and family simply as Betty. Two years later, their son Desmond was born. He died in 2004 in England. John's lungs had never really improved. On many occasions, Helena had to erect a tent in the back garden of their house in Glasnevin so as John could go out and sit in it in order to try and get some fresh air into his lungs. He regularly attended a clinic in Dublin run by French nuns. In June 1925, at the young age of thirty-five, the effects of German gas finally caught up with John and he died. He left behind a young family and a grief-stricken wife. Further tragedy struck Helena when their second son, named James, died a few months after John died.

Private John Smith and his wife Helena.

To survive through the dark depressing years of the twenties and thirties in Dublin, Helena had to do with odd jobs in order to rear her daughter and son. Despite the fact that John died from war-wounds, Helena laboured hard to get an army pension from the British authorities and eventually got one. In her spare time, she worked voluntarily for the Royal British Legion in Dublin, who looked after thousands of Irish veterans of that terrible war. Her daughter, Betty, followed in her mother's footsteps, and she too was a voluntary worker for the Legion in Dublin for many years. Helena and Betty were regular attenders at the November Remembrance Services held at Islandbridge on the banks of the River Liffey. There were times, according to Betty, her mother *'cried her eyes out at the Service'* thinking of her husband John. She simply never forgot him. On 15 July 1976, Helena died at the great age of eighty-five. She was buried beside her beloved husband John in the cemetery at St. Mobhi's in Glasnevin, Dublin. May they both rest in peace. In 2004, Betty retired from her voluntary work at the British Legion.(38)

Two of those English-born lads who died at Mouse Trap Farm on 24 May 1915 were 16693 Private George Amos and 16694 Private George Alderson. The first thing to notice is their Regimental Numbers, one follows the other. The two Georges, along with another English man named James Unsworth, came from Durham. At the outbreak of the War, they went to their local recruiting office in Newcastle-on-Tyne and tried to enlist into the Durham Light Infantry or The Green Howards. Such was the eagerness to enlist amongst the young men from the mining area of Wheatley Hill, the three lads were told at the recruiting office that both regiments had filled their quotas and that they should come back in a few weeks to try again. Not content to hang about for a few weeks and miss all the action, the three lads decided to enlist into the Royal Dublin Fusiliers. After twelve weeks of square- and ear-bashing from instructors, the two Georges were posted to the 2nd Dublins and James was posted to the 1st Dublins. Before he left for France, George Amos became engaged to a local girl from Wheatley Hill. The other George, i.e. George Alderson, was married to a Miss Hannah Simpson from Thornley in Durham. George Amos and George Alderson, two young English lads who joined the Dublin Fusiliers together, died together at Mouse Trap Farm on 24 May 1915. They were both twenty-one years of age. The third of these likely lads, although not as much of a lad as his two mates, Pte. James Unsworth, was killed in Gallipoli on 29 June 1915. He too was married and was forty-one when he died. George Amos's fiancée never married, she died in 1999.(39) The bodies of these three Durham men who died with the Dublin Fusiliers were never found. Both George Alderson and George Amos's names are mentioned in the Dublin Fusiliers panel on the Menin Gate at Ieper. James Unworth's name is on the Helles Memorial at Cape Helles in Gallipoli.

Hugh Patrick Shine was a young Second Lieutenant with the 1st Royal Irish Fusiliers, He was killed at Mouse Trap Farm on 24 May as well. Hugh was one of three Shine brothers who were officers in the regular army before the outbreak of war. All three were ex-pupils in the prestigious Benedictine Downside Abbey near Bath in England. All three were killed in the War. Their father was Colonel J.M.F Shine, C.B., a Royal Army Medical Corps Doctor. Their mother was Kathleen Mary Shine who, according to family beliefs, died from a broken heart in 1924. The Shine family lived, and still live, at Abbeyside, Dungarvan, Co. Waterford.(40)

The first of the Shine brothers who died was 2nd Lieut. John Denis Shine of the 1st Royal Irish Regiment. John was born on 10 September 1894 and went to Downside in September 1905. *'Gozo'* Shine, as he was called by his schoolmates, distinguished himself in all the school sports. He was awarded a First Eleven colours in the schools cricket, association football and hockey teams. He also became a sergeant in the school's Officer Training Corps and was a member of the School's Library Committee. In 1912, he passed into Sandhurst and the following year was commissioned into the Royal Irish Regiment. When war broke out, he went to France with his regiment and was wounded in the groin at Mons on 27 August 1914. He was carried away to a neighbouring church that was used as a hospital. Almost immediately after his arrival the building was destroyed by shellfire, killing all those in it. John died within a few days of his twentieth birthday.(41) He is buried at Mons Communal Cemetery, Grave reference IV.B.18.

The second of the Shine family that died was 2nd Lieut. Hugh Patrick. As already stated he died at Mouse Trap Farm on 24 May 1915. Hugh was the youngest of the three brothers to die. Born on 20 August 1896, he went to Downside in September 1905. *'Full of energy'*, wrote his school's account of him. Like his older brother, Hugh was a keen sportsman. He represented his house, Carvel, at cricket, hockey and golf. He also achieved the rank of Lance Corporal in the school's OTC. In December 1913, Hugh left Downside and followed his brother to Sandhurst. On 21 May 1915, Hugh wrote to the Headmaster at Downside mentioning several *'Old Gregorians'*, contemporaries of his own, whom he had met in France, some of whom had since been killed. The letter concluded with the words: '*It does not seem as if there will be many left when the war is over.*' (42) Three days later he died himself. He was eighteen years of age. Hugh's name is on the Menin Gate Panel 42.

The third and final tragedy to hit Col. Shine and his wife Kathleen was the death of their eldest son James Owen. Captain James Owen Williams Shine was an officer in the 1st Battalion of the Royal Dublin Fusiliers. Born on 23 April 1891, he was the first of the Shine boys to attend Downside in September 1902. He was described as '*an able boy, gifted with considerable eloquence and humour*' qualities that enabled him to become a successful actor on the Downside stage. In 1906, he passed the Lower Certificate, and

2nd Lieutenant John Denis Shine.
1st Royal Irish Regiment, killed near Mons, 27 August 1914.

he passed the Higher Certificate in each of the following three years. In 1909, he passed into Sandhurst and, on completion of his course at the Military College, was gazetted to the Royal Dublin Fusiliers.43) He joined his battalion in India and on their return to England he was transferred to the 2nd Battalion. Luckily he missed the terrible ordeal at Gallipoli. He was wounded in the leg in July 1916 at the Battle of the Somme and, following his recovery, he returned to the Front and joined the 9th Royal Dublin Fusiliers on 8 October 1916 to take command of 'C' Company who at that time were in Loker. Between April and the middle of June 1917, he worked as a Staff Officer with the 16th (Irish) Division. This was a vital time for the Division in their preparation for their attack on Wijtschate, which began at dawn on 7 June 1917. During that battle, the 2nd, 8th and 9th Royal Dublin Fusiliers were kept in reserve. Their turn for front-line assault came on 16 August when they attacked the German machine-gun pits at the Potsdam,

2nd Lieutenant Hugh Patrick Shine.
1st Royal Irish Fusiliers, killed near Mouse Trap Farm, 24 May 1915.

Capt. Jim Shine.
1st Royal Dublin Fusiliers, killed at Frezenberg Ridge, 16 August 1917.

Vampir and Borry Farms just east of Frezenberg. It was during this ill-fated attack that Captain Jim Shine was killed along with seven fellow officers from his battalion.(44) Also killed in that attack was their chaplain, Fr. Willie Doyle, S.J. Jim was twenty-seven years of age and is remembered on the Tyne Cot Memorial, Zonnebeke in Western Flanders, Belgium.

In reality, as an Irish battalion, the Second Battle of Ieper marked the end of the 2nd Battalion of the Royal Dublin Fusiliers. Combined with the terrible losses the 1st Battalion of the Dublins suffered in Gallipoli during the month of April 1915, the grief inflicted upon the people of Dublin must have been shattering. Regardless of any political reasons, on a human level, was it any wonder why, one year later, the Easter Rising in Dublin was initially unpopular amongst the people of the City.

No attempt was made to retake Mouse Trap Farm until the Third Battle of Ieper, which began two years later on 31 July 1917. The Second Battle of Ieper effectively ended on the 24 May 1915. In reducing the Ieper salient to a flat curve east of the city, the Germans had achieved their greatest success of the year. A shortage of troops and ammunition had prevented them from making the major breakthrough they had planned. The overall British losses in the battle from 24 April to 31 May were 2,150 officers and 57,125 other ranks. French estimates of their own casualties were 10,000. The overall German losses were 850 officers and 34,073 other ranks. The majority of the Dublin Fusiliers who died are amongst the 54,896 names on the Menin Gate at Ieper, Panels 44-46.

Unlike the Canadians, who have a beautiful memorial at St. Julien, there is no memorial specifically to the Irishmen who died around St. Julien and Mouse Trap Farm in April and May of 1915. On Monday morning, 4 September 2000, fifty-nine members and friends of the Royal Dublin Fusiliers Association made an historic visit to Mouse Trap Farm. The visit was kindly arranged through Dr. Jim Stacey, Dungarvan Great War Society, Mr. Geert Spillebeen, a Belgian radio journalist, Mr. Robert Missinne, school teacher at St. Julien, Mr. Erwin Ureel, a Warrant Officer in Belgian Army and friend of the RDF Assoc. Thanks must also go to Mr. Johan Vandelanotte and Mrs. Trees Vanesste, executives from VVV Heuvelland Tourist Office in Kemmel.

The present farmhouse is built in front of where the old farmhouse once stood. This was reduced to rubble in the attack on 24 May 1915. The farm is run by a young farmer and his wife, and out of respect for their privacy their name shall remain with the author. After introductions were made, a brief story was told of the terrible events that occurred nearby by Mr. Tom Burke and Mr. Brian Moroney from the RDF Assoc. Mr. Robert Missinne kindly gave the gathering a brief account of his research into the events of April and May 1915. Robert is a schoolteacher at St. Julien and has a particular interest in the gas attack at Mouse Trap Farm. He had brought along his class of young boys and girls aged between ten and twelve years of age to take part in the remembrance ceremony. Our ceremony began with the naming of ten Dublin Fusiliers who died in the gas attacks. Ten members of the RDFA group each read out one name, address and age of an Irish soldier who had died at this very sacred place.

In many ways, naming these men returned to them a sense of identity, dignity and respect. It was perhaps a belated funeral. Following this very emotive part of our ceremony, two members of our association laid poppy wreaths on the gable end of the farmhouse. The farmer had put hooks in the wall in preparation. Written in the centre of one of the wreaths was Wilfred Owen's poem *Dulce et Decorum est*.

Belgian school children at Mouse Trap Farm on the 4th September 2000.

The other wreath was laid by Mr. Kevin Cunningham, a friend of the family of Sgt. William Malone, 2nd Royal Dublins who died at the Farm in May 1915. Sgt. William Malone came from Grantham Street off Dublin's South Circular Road. He was a married man; his wife Rose Cox came from Brannockstown near Trim in Co. Meath. *See Footnote*. After the wreaths were laid, we said a decade of the Rosary and offered the Lord's Prayer that was led by Mr. Pat Cummins of the RDF Assoc. The final act of our service was one that I will never forget. Almost all the men and women in our group displayed emotion. With Robert and his teaching colleague playing their guitars, the school children began to sing a song of peace in English. It was simply beautiful. If only those poor men who died nearby all those years ago could see and hear those Belgian children singing in their honour, how proud they would have been. After the song, folks just stood in silence for a while then made their way to thank the children for their lovely singing. Some day I hope Irish children will go to this place and sing a song of peace.

Sgt. William Malone, 2nd Royal Dublin Fusiliers.
Killed in action 24 May 1915 at Mouse Trap Farm.

Our visit to Mouse Trap Farm was probably the first time since the war ended that a group of Irish people went there to remember their fallen countrymen. We concluded the formalities with the presentation to our new friends at Mouse Trap Farm a picture of the Dublin Fusiliers Arch in St. Stephen's Green, Dublin. We cannot thank them enough for allowing us to visit their home. Two days later our bus passed by the farm on our way to Ieper and the wreaths were still on the farmhouse wall. I had a little thought to myself as the bus passed the farm. 'Till the next time lads, all the best. You were not forgotten. My only regret is that it took so long for us to remember and acknowledge you.

Footnote
During the Easter Rising, William Malone's brother Michael was killed fighting with the Irish volunteers against the Sherwood Foresters at No. 25 Northumberland Road in Dublin. (Interestingly, Willie and Michael's sister, Brigid Malone, married another Irish rebel named Dan Breen). Was there ever a more poignant example of the tragedy of Irish history in the fact that here was two men from the same Irish family who died in battles they believed were for just causes? There is no logic in saying they fought on opposing sides. Irish history is too complicated to present their deaths in such simple terms. There is a memorial plaque to Michael Malone of the Irish Volunteers on the house at No. 25 Northumberland Road, Dublin. His brother, Sgt. William Malone, now has a brass memorial plaque at Mouse Trap Farm in Flanders.

A week or so after the Rising had ended; a first anniversary death notice was placed in *The Irish Independent* newspaper on 6 May 1916 that read:

> In sad and loving memory of my dear husband Sgt. William Malone, 2nd Royal Dublin Fusiliers, who was killed in action at St. Julien on May 24th 1915. Sweet heart of Jesus have mercy on his soul... Inserted by his loving wife and children.

Above Mrs. Malone's notice in *The Irish Independent* was a notice from Mrs. McDonnell asking for the people of Dublin to pray for her three sons. The Easter Rising in Dublin occurred roughly one year after the Gallipoli landings and the gas attack at St. Julien. The people who lived in the inner streets of Dublin city had not yet recovered from the terrible loss of loved ones resulting from those attacks. There is a fascinating twist of history in the placement of this brass plaque to Sgt. Willie Malone at Mouse Trap Farm. The gun used by Michael Malone to inflict terrible casualties on British soldiers at Northumberland Road in Easter Week 1916 was nicknamed 'Peter the Painter' (See Reference 45). It was a nine millimetre Mauser pistol with a shoulder stock. The gun was lent to Malone by Eamon De Valera prior to the attack later known as the Battle of Mount Street Bridge. During the early 1970s, the De Valera family handed the gun, along with four others, into Garda safekeeping. Ironically enough, on Thursday 24 May 1999, 'Peter the Painter' was handed over to the National Museum of Ireland by the then Garda Commissioner, Mr. Eugene Crowley, in the presence of members of the De Valera family.

Volunteer Michael Malone, Irish Volunteers.
Killed in action Easter Week April 1916.

Describing the gun as a 'sinister weapon', Master Terry de Valera said it had been taken as a trophy of war by the British but the officer in question had returned it to his (Master de Valera's) father many year later.(45) To add further irony, the Irish brass-works company who cast and produced the bronze relief of the Battle of Mesen now on display in the Island of Ireland Peace Park at Mesen, was a Dublin company named Kilmainham Art Foundry Ltd. The brass plaque to Sgt. Malone was designed and cast by the owner of Kilmainham Art Foundry Ltd, a man named Willie Malone, the grandson of Sgt. Willie Malone of the 2nd Royal Dublin Fusiliers who died at Mouse Trap Farm in May 1915.

Cemeteries in which are buried men from the Royal Dublin Fusiliers.
Some of whom died near Ieper in the Winter and Spring of 1914 / 1915 and from the gas attacks at St. Julien, Ieper, in April and May 1915.

Ploegsteert Memorial. This memorial stands in the Berks Cemetery Extension that is located 12.5 kilometres south of Ieper town centre on the N365 leading from Ieper to Mesen (Messines), to Ploegsteert and on to Armentieres. From Ieper town centre, the Rijselsestraat runs from the market square, through the Lille Gate (Rijselpoort) and directly over the crossroads with the Ieper ring road. The road name then changes to Rijselseweg (N336). The N365, which forms the right hand fork, leads to the town of Mesen (Messines). The Cemetery lies three kilometres beyond Mesen on the right hand side of the N365 and opposite Hyde Park Corner Royal Berks Cemetery. The memorial is a covered circular colonnade and commemorates over 11,000 men who have no known grave. There are thirty-eight Dublin Fusiliers on this memorial of which there are two, nineteen-year-old Dublin Fusiliers listed. They are Pte. Jeremiah Shirley from Nelson Street, Athy, Co. Kildare and Lance-Cpl. John Sullivan whose parents lived in Borris, Co. Carlow. John was killed in June 1918.

Bailleul Communal Cemetery. Bailleul is a large town in France near the Belgian border. It is 14.5 kilometres south-west of Ieper and on the main road from St. Omer to Lille. From the Grand Place, take the Ieper road and 400 metres along this road is a sign indicating the direction of the cemetery. Turn down right into a small road and follow for approximately 400 metres; the cemetery is on the right. There are only eight Dublins buried in this cemetery. However there are forty Dublin Fusiliers buried in the Bailleul Communal Cemetery Extension. The youngest is seventeen year old Pte. Thomas Gerald McCormac from Portsmouth. He had previously served in the Royal Munster Fusiliers, which meant he joined up very young, possibly giving a false date of birth upon enlistment.

Prowse Point Military Cemetery. The cemetery is located 11.5 kilometres south of Ieper town-centre on the road leading from Rijselseweg N365, which connects Ieper to Wijtschate, Mesen, Ploegsteret on to Armentieres. From Ieper town-centre, the Rijselsestraat runs from the market square, through the Lille Gate (Rijselpoort) and directly over the crossroads with the Ieper ring road. The road name then changes to the Rijselseweg. Head for Wijtschate and Mesen. Take the road out of Mesen that leads past The Island of Ireland Peace Park. Two kilometres after Mesen is the left hand turning onto Rue St. Yvon. The cemetery is located 600 metres along this road on the right hand side. The Cemetery was begun by the 2nd Royal Dublin Fusiliers and the 1st Royal Warwicks and was used from November 1914 to April 1918. It was named after Brigadier General C.B. Prowse D.S.O (Somerset Light Infantry) who was killed in July 1916. There are forty-six Dublin Fusiliers buried in this cemetery. The youngest is Pte. James Connolly aged eighteen from 9 Tyrell's Place, Fitzgibbon Street, Dublin. Also buried here is Pte. Christopher Rogers from Woodroofes Cottages, Islandbridge, Dublin. A married man with a young family, Christopher lived at 10 Vancies Buildings in Bishop Street, Dublin. In November 1998, a nephew of Christopher laid a wreath at his grave. It was the first time any member of his family had done so since he was buried there.

The Menin Gate Memorial: Ieper is a town in the Province of West Flanders. The Memorial is situated at the eastern side of the town on the road to Menin and Courtrai (Kortrijk) and bears the names of men who were lost without trace during the defence of the Ieper salient in the Great War. There are over 54,896 names of officers and other ranks engraved on the Portland Stone. There are 460 Royal Dublin Fusiliers on Panels 44 and 46. Each night at 8:00 p.m. the traffic under the memorial is stopped and the local Fire Brigade sound the Last Post. The three McDonnell brothers are listed on this memorial. The youngest Dublin Fusilier on the memorial is sixteen-year-old Pte. Myles Mahoney from 10 Lower Bridge Street, Dublin.

A time to remember

Mrs. Marjorie Quarton.
The Royal Dublin Fusiliers Association.

One lady member of the Royal Dublin Fusiliers Association who was present at Mouse Trap Farm in a return visit by the RDFA in September 2002 was Mrs. Marjorie Quarton. Her father, Captain Standish Smithwick fought at the farm with the 2nd Dublins in May 1915 and later in August 1917 at Frezenberg Ridge. She wrote the following account of her very emotional experience on returning to the places where her father had once been in a terrible war.

Mrs. Marjorie Quarton at Mouse Trap Farm
on Saturday 7 September 2002.

A young Standish Smithwick. Royal Dublin Fusiliers.

My father.

'Did you enjoy your holiday?' my friends asked. It's hard to say. The weekend trip in September for members of the Royal Dublin Fusiliers Association to Flanders was certainly enjoyable, in that the company was great, the hotels comfortable and the food as good as it was ample. I felt emotionally drained at times.

My father, Standish Smithwick, was born in Ireland in 1878 and was a regular soldier. He served in the 1st Battalion Royal Dublin Fusiliers through the Boer War, in Egypt, India and elsewhere, and re-founded the

Camel Corps in the Sudan. When the Great War broke out, he had been transferred to the 2nd Battalion. *(The Old Toughs)* and he served on the Western Front throughout, being one of only four officers to survive in the whole regiment, although severely wounded in 1915 and gassed twice, losing a lung.

At the famous Christmas truce in 1914, he met a young German who approached him and, indicating a fresh scar on Father's face said, '*I did that, I am glad I did not kill you.*' The two men had much in common, although my father was senior by several years. Both kept horses, had the same kind of background and education, were good at sports and athletics. The young man, Sigmund or Siegmund, came from Hanover. He showed father his rifle, with its telescopic sight. Both were humane men and returned to the business of trying to kill one another with disgust. Some months later, the Dublins approached Mouse Trap (or Shell Trap) Farm. Father went to investigate the buildings before it was light, suspecting that there might be snipers or hidden machine guns. Going round the end of the main building, revolver in hand, he came face to face with Sigmund, also holding his revolver, on exactly the same mission. Both stopped a yard apart. Nothing was said. Then, each turned his back and walked away, frightened no doubt, but fairly sure that he would not be shot.

Father didn't talk about the war in later years, except in general terms. But, as an old man, during his last illness, he relived the incident many times and the gas attack that followed – the first of the war.

After the war.

In 1918, my father was made second-in-command of Catterick Camp in Yorkshire with the rank of Lieut.-Col. He and his first wife lived in Richmond, Yorkshire. He was then sent to Constantinople. When the regiment was disbanded in 1922, he was transferred to the Duke of Cornwall's Light Infantry and sent to India. His wife, Dolly, died and was buried at sea on her way to join him there in 1922. He served with the D.C.L.I., mainly in India, until he retired in 1928. He didn't enjoy his time in the D.C.L.I. He was given a clerical job in the War Office which he hated. A year later he married my mother Marjorie Cooper. He was awarded the military O.B.E. and retired to Ireland. The twenties had been a bad time for an officer in the British Army to retire to his Irish home, the country having been torn by Civil War just a few years before. Many felt they had no future here.

However, my father was delighted when he inherited the family home, Crannagh, near Nenagh in Co Tipperary. The couple moved there after their marriage in May 1929 and I, their only child, was born eighteen months later. The place was run down and money was scarce, but Father was a born farmer, with an instinctive knowledge of livestock. He was a noted horseman and high handicap polo player in his day and had loathed city life. The Economic War broke many Irish farmers, but he just about survived. I never remember him in really good health, as he was full of splinters of metal, resulting from a grenade explosion that shattered his rifle in 1915. For years, he suffered from bouts of agonising pain as the splinters moved about in his body. Finally, one of them pierced his stomach wall and he died of internal bleeding on 10 April 1958, aged eighty. During the six weeks illness before his death, he dreamed and raved in delirium about the Great War. In particular, he relived his second meeting with the young soldier he had met during the Christmas truce of 1914 and the approach to the Frezenberg Ridge, where he was left for dead after being gassed.

He and my mother, who died 29 May 1979, are buried in Monsea graveyard, four miles from Nenagh. His only request to me when he knew he was dying was to put 'Royal Dublin Fusiliers' in full, on his headstone, which I did.

A Prayer.

The following is a prayer which my father, Capt. Standish Smithwick, carried with him throughout the war.

Let me not pray to be sheltered from dangers
But to be fearless in facing them.
Let me not beg for the stilling of my pain
But for the heart to conquer it.
Let me not look for allies in life's battlefield
But to my own strength.
Let me not crave in anxious fear to be saved
But hope for the patience to win my freedom.
Grant me that I may not be a coward,
Feeling your mercy in my success alone:
But let me find the grasp of your hand in my failure.

(Rabindranath Tagore. Trans. from *The Bengali*)

References.

1. For a more detailed account of the action around the Farm Phillipeaux after which later became known amongst The Faughs as *'Sydney Street'*, see Amanda Moreno and David Truesdale. *Angels and Heroes. The Story of a machine gunner with the Royal Irish Fusiliers August 1914 to April 1915.* Published by the Royal Irish Fusiliers Museum in Armagh. 2004 Pp. 59-62.

2. War Diary 2nd Battalion Royal Dublin Fusiliers. August 1914- November 1916. PRO London. WO95 / 1481.

3. Liddle Hart. B.H. *The Real War 1914-1918.* Faber and Faber. London. p 145.

4. British Commission for Military History. *Look to the Front. Studies in the First World War.* Spellmount Ltd, Kent, 1999. Article written by Edward M Spiers. *Chemical Warfare in the First World War.* p 163, *The Times* 29th April 1915.

5. Ibid. p 164.

6. Gilbert. M. *First World War.* Weidenfeld and Nicholson, London. 1994. p 197.

7. Neillands. R. *The Great War Generals on the Western Front. 1914-19.* Robinson, London. 1999. p 149.

8. Ibid. p 150.

9. Gilbert. M. *First World War.* p 145.

10. War Diary 2nd Battalion Royal Dublin Fusiliers. PRO London. WO95 / 1481.

11. Wylly, C.B. Col H. C. *Crown and Company The Historical Records of the 2nd Battalion Royal Dublin Fusiliers. Vol. II. 1911-1922.* Schull Books, Cork. 2000. p 40.

12. *Angels and Heroes.* Pp. 105-106.

13. War Diary 2nd Battalion Royal Dublin Fusiliers. PRO London. WO95 / 1481.

14. Geoghegan. C.B. Brig. Gen. S. *The Campaigns and History of The Royal Irish Regiment.* Vol. II. 1900 to 1922. p 78.

15. *Angels and Heroes.* p 108.

16. Wylly, C.B. Col H. C. *Crown and Company The Historical Records of the 2nd Battalion Royal Dublin Fusiliers.* p 42.

17. Geoghegan. C.B. Brig. Gen. S. *The Campaigns and History of The Royal Irish Regiment.* p 78.

18. Wylly, C.B. Col H. C. *Crown and Company The Historical Records of the 2nd Battalion Royal Dublin Fusiliers.* p 41.

19. Casualty statistics study carried out by author on the 2nd Royal Dublin Fusiliers. Combination of data contained from CWGC and Soldiers Died Series. Part 73. HMSO London. 1921.

20. *Angels and Heroes.* p 107.

21. *Soldiers Died Series.* CD Rom. Naval and Military Press 1998. Version 1.1. And Geoghegan. p 78.

22. Casualty statistics study carried out by author on the 2nd Royal Dublin Fusiliers. Combination of data contained from CWGC and Soldiers Died Series. Part 73. HMSO London. 1921.

23. Family papers of Private Hugh Lynch, 2nd Battalion, Royal Dublin Fusiliers. Available from RDF Assoc.

24. War Diary 2nd Battalion Royal Dublin Fusiliers. PRO London. WO95 / 1481.

25. Ibid.

26. Geoghegan. C.B. Brig. Gen. S.-
The Campaigns and History of The Royal Irish Regiment. p 31.

27. War Diary 2nd Battalion Royal Dublin Fusiliers. PRO London. WO95 / 1481. Report on events of 24 May 1915.

28. Ibid.

29. Ibid.

30. Diffley. S. *The Men in Green. The Story of Irish Rugby.* Pelham Books London. 1973. p 68-71.

31. War Diary 2nd Battalion Royal Dublin Fusiliers. PRO London. WO95 / 1481. Report on events of 24 May 1915.

32. Letter written to Mrs Loveband from Mrs Digby Johnson. This letter was given to Mr. Tom Burke, RDF Assoc by Mrs. Marjorie Quarton from Nenagh, Co. Tipperary. The typed letter was among her father's papers Capt. Standish Smithwick. 2nd Royal Dublin Fusiliers.

33. War Diary 2nd Battalion Royal Dublin Fusiliers. PRO London. WO95 / 1481. Report on events of 24 May 1915.

34. Geoghegan. C.B. Brig. Gen. S.
The Campaigns and History of The Royal Irish Regiment. p 31.

35. War Diary 2nd Battalion Royal Dublin Fusiliers. PRO London. WO95 / 1481.

36. Casualty statistics study carried out by author on the 2nd Royal Dublin Fusiliers. Combination of data contained from CWGC and Soldiers Died Series. Part 73. HMSO London. 1921.

37. Private collection of Mr Michael Lee. RTE, Donnybrook, Dublin 4. See also RDF Assoc. CD titled *Remembering the Great War.* Available from RDF Assoc.

38. Conversation between Tom Burke and Miss Helena Smith, daughter of Private John Smith, 2nd Royal Dublin Fusiliers.

39. Family papers of Mrs. Marian Hughes from Gravesend, niece of Private George Amos. Mrs. Hughes told her father's story to Mr. Pat Hogarty, RDF Assoc.

40. Family papers of Mr. Jim Shine, Dungarvan, Co. Waterford.

41. *Downside and the War. 1914-1919*. Published by the College in London in 1925. p 83.

42. Ibid. p 112.

43. Ibid. p 178.

44. War Diary 9th Battalion Royal Dublin Fusiliers. PRO London. WO95 /1974.

45. *The Irish Times* 24 May 1990. Peter the Painter was a nine millimetre Mauser pistol with a shoulder stock.

The title, Peter the Painter, originated from the siege of a house in London in January 1911. On 17 December 1910, a jeweller's shop, H.S. Harris in Houndsditch, was burgled at night. A neighbour notified the police. Three unarmed policemen confronted the burglars. All three policemen were shot and killed. Warrants for the arrest of the burglars went out with posters of the three suspects. Two weeks later on 2 January 1911, a Mrs. Gershwin of 100 Sidney Street reported at Arbor Square Police Station that three men answering the description of the wanted men had hired a room at her house. The next morning, police surrounded the house. The three men, who were Russian anarchists, refused to surrender and a gun battle ensued, Winston Churchill, the then Home Secretary, summoned the Scots Guards in full battle dress to dislodge the men. By late afternoon the house was alight. The bodies of two of the anarchists were found charred. However, the body of the third suspect, Peter Piatkov, subsequently nicknamed Peter the Painter, was never found. It seems the memory of the Siege of Sidney Street was ripe in the minds of men from the 1st Royal Irish Fusiliers when, in October 1914, they had to burn a farm house named Farm Phillipeaux near Armentieres in France that contained defiant German soldiers. Following the battle to take the farmhouse, the Royal Irish Fusiliers named the burnt-out farmhouse, Sidney Street. By a further coincidence Peter the Painter and an Irish Sidney Street type incident occurred during the 1916 Easter Rising in Dublin when British Soldiers again had to burn a house at No. 25 Northumberland Road from which Volunteer Michael Malone and his comrades had made a defiant stand. Malone used a Peter the Painter pistol in his fight with the British soldiers. It would seem that fires, shoot-outs and sieges were synonymous with Peter the Painter. Perhaps, just as the mysterious Peter Piatkov would like to have been remembered.

Note: CWGC is the abbreviation for Commonwealth War Graves Commission. Website: www.cwgc.org.

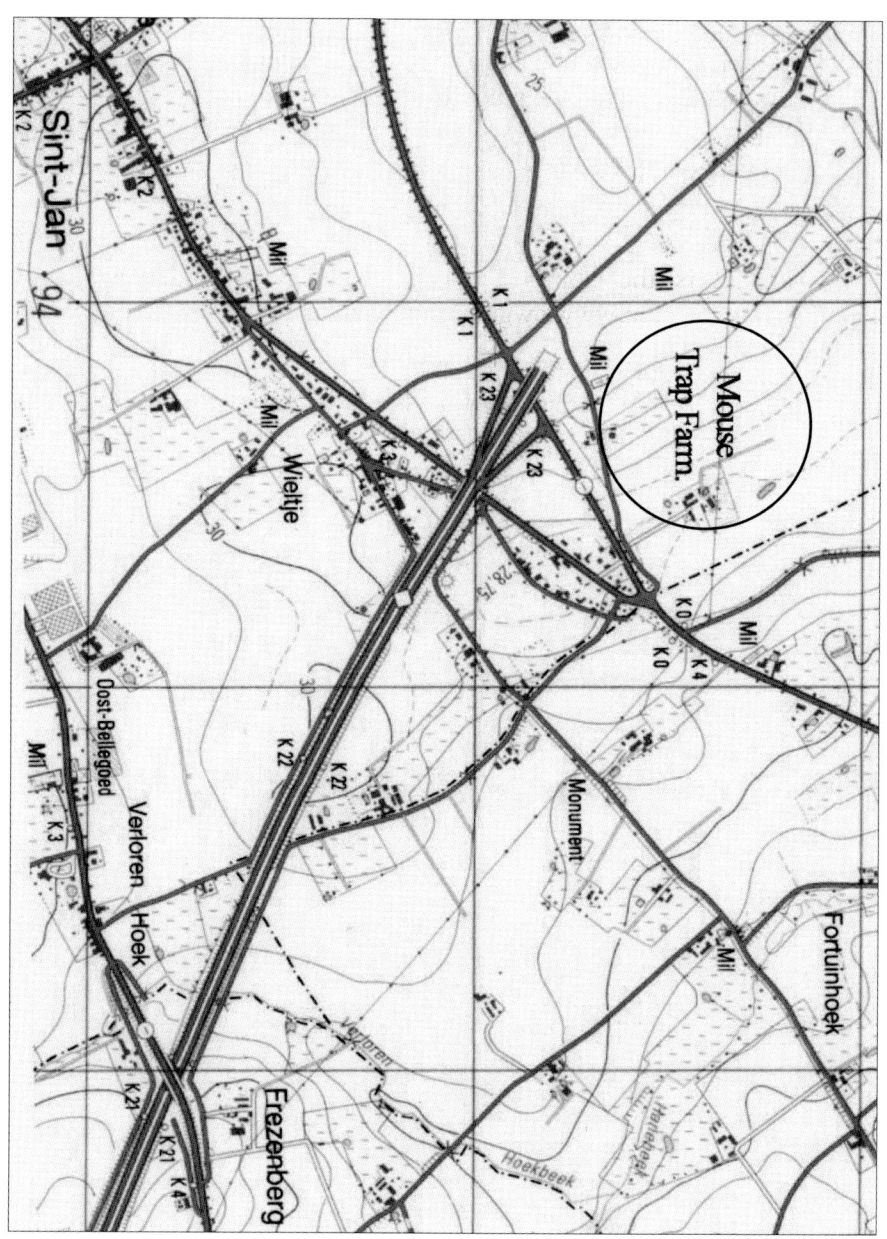

Mouse Trap Farm, June 2001. Ieper is Southwest of Sint-Jan.
Copyright National Geographic Institute Belgium. 28 / 1-2

Notes

Notes

Notes